EYEWITNESS

MINI MONSTERS

Written by Susan Mayes
Illustrated by Gary Boller

HENDERSON

An imprint of DK Publishing, Inc.

THE WORLD OF MINI MONST

Do things that scuttle, buzz, flutter, or slither give you the heebie-jeebies? Do they make you squirm with horror and delight at the same time?

BEAUTIFUL BUGS AND SLIMY SLUGS

This book reveals a multitude of mini monsters in detailed close-up for you to study and wonder at. Things that jump and fly and sting and swarm...they're all here. We even reveal the hidden horrors of mini monsters that lurk in your home!

Why do these little beasts look the way they do? Where do they live? What do they eat? How do they protect themselves? Do they have any horrible habits? Just remember...this is their world you're looking into, so what seems odd or slightly nasty to you is really only nature at work!

INSECT BITS AND PIECES

Many people think that any small creature that creeps and crawls is called an insect, but in fact an insect is a type of creature with special characteristics. Insects have six legs, and a skeleton on the outside of their body. Weird, huh? They have three parts to their body: the head, the thorax, and the abdomen. Look at the dissected jewel beetle on the next page to see what's what.

Jewel beetle

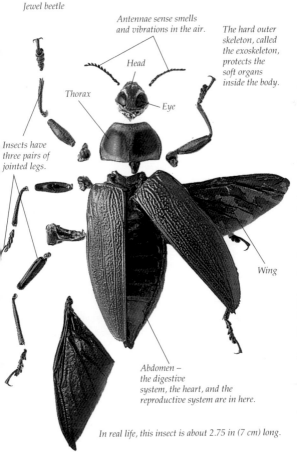

Antennae sense smells
and vibrations in the air.

Head

The hard outer
skeleton, called
the exoskeleton,
protects the
soft organs
inside the body.

Thorax

Eye

Insects have
three pairs of
jointed legs.

Wing

Abdomen –
the digestive
system, the heart, and the
reproductive system are in here.

In real life, this insect is about 2.75 in (7 cm) long.

BELIEVE IT OR NOT...

There are at least one million insect species! There are
more of this type of creature than of any other on Earth.

THE FIRST MINI MONSTERS

Insects were the first creatures ever to fly. They lived about 300 million years ago, even before dinosaurs! Most of the ancient kinds are extinct now, but many modern creepy crawlies are close relations of the oldies.

EARLY ARRIVALS
In prehistoric times, there were brightly colored, scented flowers. These attracted butterflies, bees, and other insects that lived in those days. They carried pollen from flower to flower, just as insects do today.

TRAPPED IN AMBER
We know about insects from long ago because some have been perfectly preserved in amber. This is fossilized resin that oozed from pine trees. Insects attracted by its sweetness became trapped in the sticky stuff, which then hardened and became buried for millions of years.

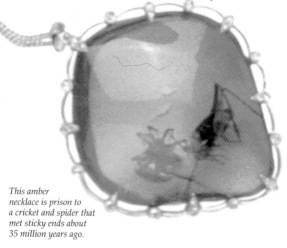

This amber necklace is prison to a cricket and spider that met sticky ends about 35 million years ago.

ROCKY REMAINS

Some insects became trapped in muddy sediment (grains of sand, soil, and plant matter) and became fossilized. Because insects are usually small and delicate, many of them rotted away before fossilization could take place, so there aren't a lot of rocky insect remains around now.

BELIEVE IT OR NOT...

This fossilized creepy crawly isn't as small as it looks here. It's a 6-ft (1.8-m) long giant – the size of a tall man! Yikes!

FANTASTIC FLIERS

Get this! Some ancient dragonflies may have had a wingspan of up to three feet (one meter)! Most modern dragonflies are much smaller... thank goodness!

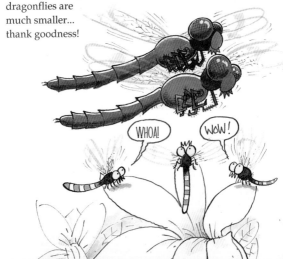

WHOA!

WOW!

SPIDERS

Spiders are not insects. They belong to a group of creepy crawlies called *arachnids*. They have eight legs and two parts to their bodies. All spiders are carnivorous (they feed on flesh!), but not all of them make webs to catch their prey. Read on if you dare!

The common garden spider's complicated web is called an orb web.

Web silk is squeezed through nozzles called spinnerets.

WONDERFUL WEBS

Some spiders make silk inside their body. They then use the silk to spin a sticky web to catch prey in. When an unsuspecting creature gets trapped, the spider runs out, wraps it in silk, and saves it for mealtime.

SUPER STRENGTH

The silk of some webs is stronger than steel wire of the same thickness.

BELIEVE IT OR NOT...
There are about 40,000 different species of spiders.

POISONOUS FANGS

Most spiders stun or kill their victims with a bite from their poisonous fangs. Very few spiders are dangerous to humans though.

FISHING NET SPIDER

This crafty hunter spins a stretchy silk net. It hangs upside down, holding the net in its four front legs, waiting to drop it over unsuspecting victims.

TEENY WEENY SPIDERS

Baby spiders are called *spiderlings*. They hatch from eggs inside a silken cocoon, then cut their way out.

BIG, HAIRY HORRORS!

Big, hairy scuttlers called tarantulas must be everybody's spider nightmare, striking fear into the hearts of the bravest people. In reality it's quite a different story. Tarantulas are shy creatures that live mainly in burrows (and you thought that only rabbits did that!). However, if you're a lizard, a mouse, or even a bird...watch out!

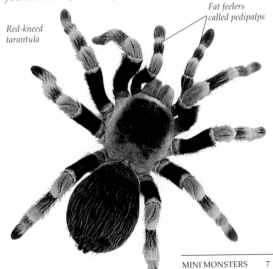

Fat feelers called pedipalps

Red-kneed tarantula

BEETLES

Beetles are the largest group of insects. There are around 300,000 different kinds around the world – in freezing cold places, in scorching hot places, in damp and muddy places – there are beetles everywhere.

BEETLE BUFFET
Beetles eat just about anything. They dine on all kinds of plants and animals, living and dead! They are often thought of as pests because they attack crops, but they do good as well, clearing up dead plants and animals.

UP, UP, AND AWAY!
Beetles have four wings. The front two are hard and strong. They cover the beetle's back and protect the long, folded wings underneath, which are used for flying.

BLISTER BEETLES
If the blood of a blister beetle gets on the skin of a person or an animal, it causes painful blisters. An excellent way of saying "Leave me alone"!

WHAT A STINK!
Now don't go upsetting this one!. The devil's coach-horse beetle defends itself by arching its tail and squirting foul-smelling liquid from its rear end. NOT a nice habit.

COLORFUL CHARACTERS

People often think of beetles as being black, but they come in all sorts of fantastic colors. Green and red are common beetle colors, but they also come in shimmering gold, bright blue, and white. Intricate patterns are another special feature of these decorative beasties.

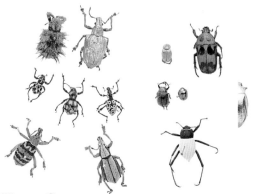

HEAVY GIANT

An adult goliath beetle can measure as long as 6 in (15 cm). Prepare to be horrified when you check this length out on a ruler.

Goliath beetle

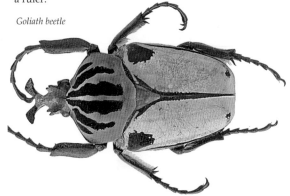

Bugs

The word "bug" is often used to describe crawling insects, but the truth is that bugs are a particular kind of crawler. They have a long, hollow feeding tube that they use to pierce food and suck up the juices. Delicious! Most bugs eat plant food, but some eat live prey!

Shield Bugs

Many of these bugs have brightly colored patterns that look a lot like decorative shields. Shield bugs are also called stink bugs because they ooze a nasty-smelling liquid when in danger. Phewee!

Assassin Bugs

This delightful creature feeds on other insects. It stabs its victims with its feeding tube and sucks out their juices. Some South American assassin bugs feed on the blood of humans.

Assassin bug feeding

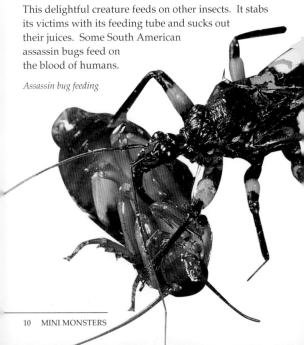

Eye Eye!

A deceptive bug this one! The front of this lantern bug's head looks like an alligator's head. When it flies, it flashes two huge false "eyes" on its wings. These probably scare off attackers. Well, it would, wouldn't it?

Lantern bug

Baby Bugs

Baby bugs look very much like their parents, only they are smaller and have no wings. Aah!

Watch Your Toes!

Giant water bugs are common in the tropics. They are also known as toe-biters, which is a tiny bit worrying! They live underwater and feed on creatures such as snails, small fish, or even frogs. So next time you go swimming in the tropics, keep your shoes on!

Slowly Does It

The water measurer is a long-legged bug that takes life easy. It moves around slowly on the surface of the water and feeds on insects that are dead or dying.

ANT ANTICS

Ants belong to a group of insects called
hymenoptera. They are called "social"
insects because they live in groups.
There can be anything from 20 to many
thousands in each group, called a *colony*.
Their homes are underground nests.

FANGS A LOT!

Ants have different jaw shapes, depending on what they
eat. The fierce-looking bulldog ant below is a *carnivore*
(meat eater). It uses its enormous, spiky jaws, called
mandibles, for chopping up other insects. Yum yum!

OKAY BOSS!

Each nest is begun by a single queen ant. She is the only
one that lays eggs. The worker ants take care of her,
search for food, and feed her. Big-jawed soldier ants keep
enemies out of the nest.

SMELLY MESSAGES

Ants pass on messages about food, enemies, and their
nest in two ways. Either they make chemicals called
pheromones, which other ants can smell, or they make
sound signals using vibrations to get the messages across.

DRIVING THROUGH

Driver ants move their nests from place to place. The whole colony marches along, catching all the insects they can find on the way.

HONEYPOT ANTS

Honeypot ants live in semi-desert areas. In the rainy season, some of the workers are fed with water and nectar until their abdomens are huge and swollen. In the dry season, when food is scarce, the other ants feed off these living larders.

Honeypot ant

CUT AND CARRY

Parasol ants cut pieces off leaves and flowers with their sharp, pointed jaws. They struggle back to the nest with them and use them to grow a kind of fungus, which the ants then eat. Delicious!

Parasol ants

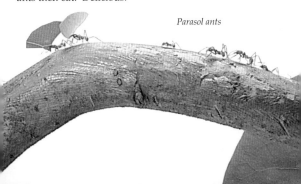

Snails and slugs are called *gastropods*, which means "belly foot." Their "belly" is really a large, flat muscular foot that can slide along. This is made easier by the slime trail that they make to help them slither smoothly.

Underneath view of a snail

Bands of muscle across the foot help push the snail forward.

BELIEVE IT OR NOT...

Most slugs and snails are male and female at the same time. The name for this is *hermaphrodite* – but two slugs or two snails still need to mate so that they can lay eggs.

BABY SNAILS

Most land snails lay eggs like little white pearls in the ground or under rotting leaves, logs, or stones. When the babies hatch out, they already have a tiny curly shell. As a snail grows, the shell grows around and around.

Uh-Oh!

A snail in danger pulls its feelers in and hides its body inside its shell.

In hot weather, a snail hides in its shell and seals the opening with a plug of slime. Cozy and safe and damp!

Tongues and Teeth

Most land snails and freshwater snails are *herbivores* (plant eaters). Their long tongue, called a *radula*, is covered with tiny sharp teeth that rasp and grate up vegetation.

Now the euglandina is a snail to be reckoned with! It's a meat eater that uses its long, sharp teeth to tear up other snails. It moves quickly when a meal is nearby and stretches out to grasp its victim. Aagh!

Believe It or Not...

The giant African snail is a monster muncher. It measures about 9 inches (23 cm) long.

This is an ordinary garden snail. What a size difference!

LOADS OF LEGS

If things with scuttling legs leave you feeling a little peculiar, then these pages are not for you! Introducing some many-legged mini monsters...

CATERPILLARS

Caterpillars are a bit short on legs compared with a few of the other characters shown here. They have six thin legs at the front of their bodies, some much fatter, sticky legs at the back, and two special ones called *claspers* at the very end.

SOW BUGS

These shy, fourteen-legged creepers like to live where it's very damp, so underneath logs, stones, and pieces of bark are good places to hunt them out.

Sow Bug

CENTIPEDES

The name "centipede" means "hundred legs," but most centipedes don't have that many (although you could spend hours trying to count them!). Centipedes are fierce hunters, with a poisonous bite, so insects and worms must beware when they hear those scuttling legs.

MILLIPEDES

These many-legged beasties have soft, pale
legs hidden underneath their body and a
very short pair of feelers at the front.
Their name means "thousand legs,"
but no millipede really has
that many.

*There are four legs in
each segment.*

*Legs move in a
wavelike pattern.*

*Despite all these legs,
millipedes meander along
very slowly.*

*Millipedes are plant eaters,
so they don't need to rush
after food.*

BELIEVE IT OR NOT...

The leggiest millipede in
the world only has 750 legs.
"Thousand legs" my foot!

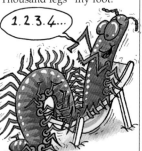

1. 2. 3. 4...

Leaps and Bounds

Legs are important to most creatures. Their uses include walking, running, digging, fighting, and, of course, jumping. Here are a few of the mini monsters whose long legs help them leap and bound around.

Leaping Locust

Look at the legs on this beastie. It's a locust and it's getting ready to leap. Its back legs are folded, ready for the high jump.

The locust's powerful leg muscles straighten out its leg joints and launch it into the air. Its wings stay closed to keep the body streamlined so the locust can get as high as possible.

When it can go no higher, the locust opens its wings as wide as it can and flaps them to carry it even farther forward.

To help it land safely, the locust spreads its legs wide, tilts its hind wings, and curves its front ones. This helps it slow down and drop gently to the ground.

FROG BEETLE

The frog beetle's back legs are long and strong, like a frog's. It uses them to leap away from enemies, then it uses its wings to fly to complete safety.

FIT AS A FLEA

Fleas are famous jumpers. They can leap as high as 12 in (30 cm). If you think that this doesn't sound very high, consider the size of a flea. That really is some high jump for a tiny creature.

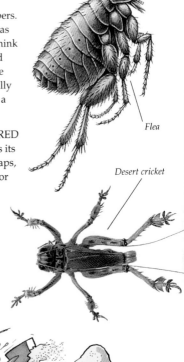

Flea

Desert cricket

HOT AND BOTHERED

The desert cricket uses its strong legs for long leaps, but it also uses them for digging. If it needs to escape from enemies or the raging heat of the midday sun, it digs speedily into the sand. It can bury itself in only a few seconds. Beat that!

EATING OUT

Mini monsters have different feeding
habits. Some can eat almost anything,
while others have more specialized
dietary requirements. Their feeding parts
suit the sort of food they dine on.

WEEVILS

Weevils have a long, curved snout called a *rostrum.*
It has tiny jaws at the end for biting small pieces
of plants.

TONGUE-TIED

Butterflies and moths have a long, tube-shaped mouth
called a *proboscis.* They hover in front of a flower to feed,
stretch out their proboscis, and delve inside for the sweet
nectar. When they are not feeding, the proboscis is coiled
up out of the way. Thank goodness for that!

*Just look at the length of this
hawk-moth's tongue!*

WOW!

TWO SETS OF CHOMPERS

Ground beetles have two pairs of jaws. One huge pair
is for chopping up worms, slugs, and other yummy
goodies. A smaller pair is for shoveling the bits into the
beetle's mouth.

AN IRON GRIP

The praying mantis grips its prey with its front legs and
uses its sharp, strong jaws for slicing it up.

A Quick Slurp

The darkling beetle lives in the desert. To get a drink, it waits until dew from early morning mist collects on its back. Then it holds its abdomen up so that the water drips down into its mouth. What a performance!

A Trail of Destruction

Caterpillars chew their way around the edges of a leaf. They grasp it between their legs, stretch out their head, then chew down toward their body. Look at the progress this common mormon caterpillar has made on a leaf. Hungry, or what?

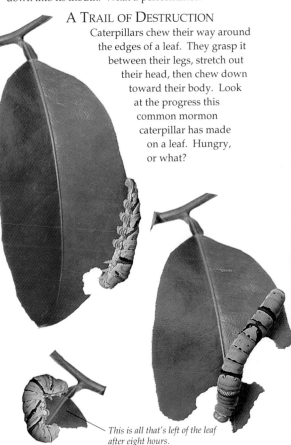

This is all that's left of the leaf after eight hours.

Yucky Habits

If you're about to munch on a tasty snack while reading these pages, a word of warning... DON'T! Some of these yucky mini monster habits will make you feel distinctly peculiar!

House-Flies

Do you ever see flies lurking around your kitchen? Well, this is what they are up to.

Spongy mouthpart

Taste buds are on the feet

When a fly smells food, it lands and tastes it with the taste buds on its feet. If it fancies the food, it spreads digestive juices on it – rather like vomiting, actually! This turns solid food mushy so the fly can dab it up with its spongelike mouthparts. That's the last time you leave food uncovered!

Germs Galore!

A mosquito feasts on blood. When it bites someone, it slurps up some of their blood, plus any germs that are in it. Then it flies on to someone else and has another meal, leaking some of the germs from the first person into the new one. This spreads the germs that cause disease.

Dung Flies

A dung fly lays its eggs in fresh droppings. When the maggots hatch out, they eat the dung. Apparently, this contains lots of nourishment for them!

YUMMY

Cave Cockroach

Cockroaches that live in caves banquet on a tasty selection of morsels. They are particularly partial to bat droppings and the remains of dead bats. Other fine food includes mites and fungi.

Live Food

The weevil-hunting wasp grasps, stings, and paralyzes weevils, but doesn't kill them. The female puts the weevils in a burrow, and lays her eggs on them. When the larvae hatch, they eat the live weevils' flesh. Ouch!

The wasp holds the weevil in position with its strong legs.

DEADLY BEASTIES

If, by some strange chance, you happen to come across any of the little horrors shown here (fairly unlikely!), the best thing you could do is RUN AWAY! They are DEADLY!

BLACK WIDOW

The female black widow spider has a bite that can kill a person. She sometimes kills her mate. Nice habit, huh?

SAHARA SCORPION

Scorpions are eight-legged relatives of spiders. They only sting to protect themselves. The Sahara scorpion is only 2.8 in (7 cm) long, but its sting is strong enough to kill you. So steer clear next time you're in the Sahara desert!

Sahara scorpion

POISONOUS SNAILS

Many seashells you find on the beach are the empty homes of sea snails. The cone shell lurks on coral reefs and stabs its prey with a poisonous dart that paralyzes and kills. A number of humans have met a sticky end in this way.

The geography cone is highly poisonous.

PRETTY DEADLY

Just in case you happen to be trekking through the jungle one day, watch out for these cute, pretty little frogs. They are called poison dart frogs. A smear of their poison can kill a human, so HANDS OFF!

This little cutie is the world's most poisonous frog.

IF YOU'RE A MALE PRAYING MANTIS...

A special warning for YOU. Beware of those crafty females you're so fond of! If they're hungry, they may eat males like you while mating.

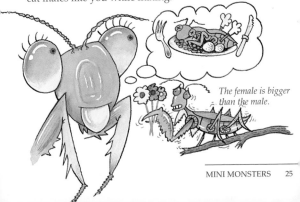

The female is bigger than the male.

Flying High

One of the main reasons why insects have survived for millions of years is that they can fly. Their wings help them escape from danger and find food and places to live.

What's In a Wing?

An insect's wings are thin and light. (Well, heavy ones wouldn't be very useful, would they?) They are stiffened by a network of veins. The flapping power comes from strong muscles in the insect's middle.

Getting Warm

Before an insect's wings can move fast enough to fly, the flight muscles need to be warmed up, especially when the weather is cool.

Mini Helicopters

Hoverflies can move forward, backward, sideways, and up and down, just like a helicopter. As their name suggests, they can also hover in midair. Very few insects can perform this stunt.

Gliding By

Some insects have wings specially made for gliding long distances. The African grasshopper has broad hind wings made for this job.

BEAUTIFUL BUTTERFLIES

Lots of tropical butterflies are big and bright. They avoid hungry enemies by darting in and out of patches of sunlight and dark, shadowy places. This makes them difficult to see.

Australian hercules moth

WONDERFUL WINGS

The Australian hercules moth has incredible wings. Its wingspan (from wingtip to wingtip) is around 10 in (25 cm). That's some flutterer!

BELIEVE IT OR NOT...

The fastest ever flier was probably a giant prehistoric dragonfly. These huge insects had to fly as fast as 43 mph (69 km/h) just to stay up in the air!

Eye Spy

Most insects are tiny, but they have more developed senses than most larger animals. They can see and hear things that humans cannot detect.

Caterpillars are surrounded by their food, so they don't need to look hard to find it. They can make do with simple eyes.

Simple Eyes

Insects that do not need sharp eyesight have eyes called *simple eyes*. These can probably only see light and shade, and not much more.

Compound Eyes

We're talking super-vision here. Beasties with *compound eyes* have excellent eyesight.

Compound eyes are made up of lots of separate sections, called *ommatidia*. The more of these there are, the more sensitive the eye is.

Huge Eyes

A dragonfly's eyes take up most of its head. This means that it can see in front, above, below, and behind, all at the same time. It's no good sneaking up on a dragonfly – it'll see you coming!

Dragonfly's head

LOTS OF EYES

Many insects have simple eyes AND compound eyes.
The wasp and the cicada both have compound eyes and
three simple eyes.

Simple eyes

Wasp

Compound eyes

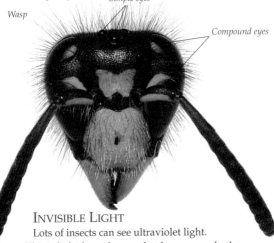

INVISIBLE LIGHT

Lots of insects can see ultraviolet light.
This is light from the sun that humans and other
animals can't see.

Some flowers have petals with lines that reflect ultraviolet
light. To an insect, this makes the lines look like bright
runways guiding them right into the middle of the flower,
where all the yummy pollen and nectar is.

HUNTING SPIDERS

Spiders that hunt for their prey have really sharp eyesight.
Well, they should really, because they have eight eyes to

spy what's happening!
This helps them stalk
their victims and pounce
on them.

Touch, Smell, and Hearin

The bodies of insects have lots of short hairs connected to their nervous system. These can feel tiny vibrations in the air made by sound and movement. Some hairs can even sense smells and flavors.

Fringed Feelers

Insects' antennae often have sensory hairs for feeling. The Indian beetle has huge, fringed antennae to help it pick up scents in the air. Beetles fan out their antennae when they fly to help them smell as much as possible.

The Indian beetle's giant antennae look like antlers.

Feathered Sensor

A male gypsy moth's big, feathered antennae are so sensitive that they can smell the scent of a female gypsy moth from far away. Moths can also tell different flowers and plants apart by their smells.

FEELING TOUCHY

Because many insects rely on touch and smell so much, they usually have small eyes, but very long antennae. The longhorn beetle has a fine pair of feelers that are jointed, so they can be moved around.

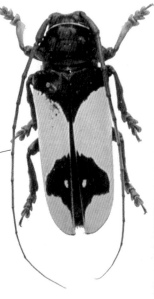

A longhorn beetle with its antennae pointing backward.

SEEING IN THE DARK

Insects that live in the dark have to use other ways of "seeing." The cave cricket lives in dark caves and feels the world around it with its long antennae.

BELIEVE IT OR NOT...

A cricket hears with its legs. Yes...really! Its ears are a swelling just below the knee on each front leg.

DOING BATTLE

Many mini monsters attack and kill the creepy crawlies they feed on. But some beasties fight their own kind to protect their territory and to compete for food and places to mate.

BATTLING BEES

Every bee colony has its own scent. If a bee from another colony tries to get into the hive, the others recognize that the intruder smells different and push it out. The intruder may curl up, telling the other bees, "I give in."

THE TALE OF THE LOST ANT

Imagine the scene...your pet cat is basking in the sunshine when an ant crawls onto its fur. Kitty gets up, stretches and wanders to another part of the neighborhood, where the ant gets off. Far from home, the ant tries to join another colony of ants. MISTAKE! The ants can smell that it's a stranger and kill it. THE END!

WHO'S BOSS?

Stag beetles compete for the dead wood that they feed and breed on. The males have big jaws that look like antlers, rather like the antlers of a real stag. They use these weapons for wrestling.

When two males meet, they stretch out their antennae to pick up lots of information about each other. Each male takes up a threatening pose to try to frighten off his opponent.

If threats don't work, each beetle tries to grip his rival around the middle, lift him up, and drop him to the ground. Sometimes, the teeth on the jaws of the winning beetle puncture the loser's tough armor.

Stag beetles

An injured beetle will probably die, especially if it lands on its back. This can be particularly bad news if there are ants around, because they enjoy a tasty beetle for supper!

UH OH!

Finding a Mate

For most creepy crawlies, a female has to mate with a male of her own kind before she can lay eggs. Finding the right mate, avoiding being eaten, and laying the eggs in a safe place is full of hazards.

Moth Mates

A moth's antennae are so sensitive to smells that it can smell the scent of a mate from far away. The Indian moon moth can smell a mate from a distance of around 6 3/4 miles (11 km) away.

Indian moon moth

Chirping Grasshoppers

A grasshopper makes a chirping sound to attract a mate. It does this by rubbing its back leg along its front wing. This makes small teeth on the leg buzz.

Courtship Dances

Just to make sure that they have found the right species to mate with, butterflies perform dancing flights. While they dance, they exchange scented chemical signals, called *pheromones*, telling them that the partner they have found is the one for them. Aaah!

LIGHTING UP

Glow-worms have nothing whatsoever to do with worms. They are the wingless females of particular kinds of beetles! At night, the female makes a light near the tip of her abdomen. This attracts males who come and mate with her. Some kinds of glow-worms even flash a code to attract a mate. Smart, aren't they?

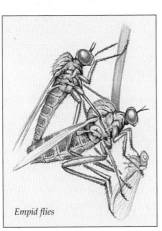

Empid flies

GORGEOUS GIFTS

In some species of insects that feed on other insects, the male gives the female a gift of food when they mate so that she doesn't eat HIM! A tasty dead insect seems to do the trick for some females. Well, they would be crazy to turn down such a special present... wouldn't they?

ALL CHANGE

For us humans, growing up is pretty straightforward compared with growing up for insects. We are born, then we grow until we become adults. But insects go through stages in which their body shape changes completely, several times, before they make it to the "grown-up" stage.

This is called *complete metamorphosis* (which means a complete change).

BUTTERFLIES

A female butterfly lays its eggs on a plant.

The eggs hatch into a squidgy-looking creature called a *larva*. A butterfly larva is called a caterpillar.

Chrysalis

Chrysalis skin splits.

Next, the caterpillar becomes something called a *pupa*, or *chrysalis*. To do this, its caterpillar skin splits to reveal its chrysalis skin underneath. The chrysalis hangs from a branch or under a leaf.

Inside the chrysalis, the butterfly's shape is forming. Many chrysalises look like old leaves. NOT very pretty!

After a few weeks the butterfly emerges from the chrysalis skin. This process takes about 20 minutes of hard work. The beautiful, new creature waits for its wings to harden properly, and then flies off to find its first meal.

LITTLE BY LITTLE

Some insects don't go through as many stages as others. They hatch from their eggs into babies called *nymphs*, which look like tiny adults.

The nymphs molt their outer skins many times, changing body size a bit each time. This is called *incomplete metamorphosis*. Insects that grow up this way include grasshoppers, cockroaches, and dragonflies.

PHEW!
I'M A GROWN-UP
AT LAST.

STINGING THINGS

If you've ever been stung by a mini monster, you'll know that it's not very pleasant! Here are some beasties with a sting in the tail.

BEES

Bees are plant eaters, so the sharp sting in their tail has nothing to do with killing prey for food – it's for scaring off enemies. But give a moment's thought to this poor little buzzer. When it stings something, the sting and part of the body tear away, and the bee dies.

WASPS

These beasties can use their sting several times, so beware! They use it for killing prey and to protect themselves. Wasps do some good though, because they kill creatures that destroy plants and fruit.

BELIEVE IT OR NOT...

About 40,000 people are killed each year by wasp or bee stings because of allergic reactions.

THE BIGGEST WASP

The tarantula hawk wasp is the world's biggest wasp. Its wingspan is about 5 in (12 cm). Aagh!

The female captures a big spider and paralyzes it with her sting. She then lays an egg on it and pushes it into a small burrow.

When the wasp grub hatches out, it feeds on the living, paralyzed spider. Live food... mmm-mmmmm!

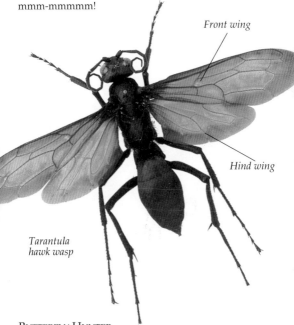

Front wing

Hind wing

Tarantula hawk wasp

BUTTERFLY HUNTER

A type of South American wasp attacks groups of butterflies sitting on the ground and collects them to make a food store for its grubs when they hatch out. After stinging the butterflies, one at a time, it bites their wings off. Nice little creature!

FALSE I.D.

Being any sort of small creature can be a dangerous business, so many little beasties have special ways of staying safe. They have sneaky ways of hiding, or they masquerade as something much more frightening.

CAMOUFLAGE

Some insects have body coloring that matches their background, making them almost impossible to see. This works best of all if they keep still...the slightest fidget and they could become supper to a hungry hunter.

Can you spot the Indian leaf butterfly? It looks just like an old leaf.

Butterfly's head

Butterfly's wing

Bottom of wing

Another type of camouflage called *disruptive coloration* disguises the body by breaking its shape up with stripes and areas of color.

IN DISGUISE

Many insects mimic (copy) the shapes and colors of things far more dangerous to scare their enemies away.

The hoverfly isn't dangerous, but it looks it because its coloring and pattern is the same as a wasp's.

The eyed hawk-moth gets its name from the big spots on its hind wings. They look like frightening, staring eyes.

Hoverfly

HOUSEHOLD HORRORS

If you thought that your home was a mini monster-free zone...WRONG! Most homes have some sort of hidden creepy crawly life. Hopefully, yours doesn't have most of these though.

COCKROACHES

These beasties are ancient insects. They live almost anywhere and eat just about everything. They can become household pests, eating any food that is left around. Their flattened bodies make it easy for them to hide in cracks, so they are difficult to get rid of.

BEDBUGS

Now these will have you scratching! Bedbugs are bloodsucking bugs. They mostly live in birds' nests and where bats roost, but they also live IN YOUR HOME! They reproduce quickly in warm conditions, so a nice warm bedroom – your mattress in particular – will make a wonderfully comfortable residence for them.

Bedbugs in close-up

Real size of a bedbug

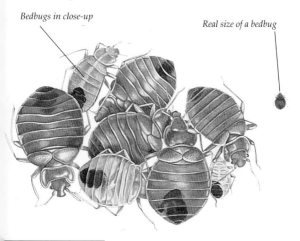

HOUSEFLIES

Every country has houseflies. These excellent fliers love to hang around your home looking for food, and they are not fussy about the quality of it either. Old leftovers will do just fine, thank you!

WASPS

Wasps often make their nests in the roofs of houses, where it's warm and safe. Ideal for the wasps maybe, but not for the humans they share the house with. Bzzzzzzzzzzz!

FLEAS

Each kind of flea prefers the blood of one sort of animal or bird. The bad news is that fleas can be smuggled into your home on an innocent pet. The good news is that animal fleas have to be very hungry to attack a human.

A flea bite leaves you with an itchy red spot. Beware of madly scratching pets!

HEAD LICE

These tiny terrors can live in human hair. They grip on tightly and puncture the skin with their mouthparts so they can suck up blood. Eeeeek!

DEATHWATCH BEETLE

These beetles feed on the wood of trees. They are the dreaded enemies of people who live in houses with timbers, as they munch away on the wood. This weakens the framework of the house.

Nests

Some insects live on their own, but others live together in groups, or *societies*. They are called *social insects* and they build nests in which they protect each other and bring up their babies. How civilized!

Wasps

The boss of a wasp colony is the queen. In the spring she begins a new nest made from chewed-up wood. She builds a few cells for her eggs.

The queen builds more paper layers around the cells to make an extra-safe and warm home.

Inside, the queen lays a single egg in each cell. When the larvae hatch out, the queen feeds them with tasty morsels of caterpillar.

The first babies grow up and become workers. They gather food for the next group of larvae. By summer, the nest may have as many as 500 wasps inside. Yikes!

ANTS

Different kinds of ants build different kinds of nests. Wood ants build enormous ones from the remains of plants. Inside, there is a complicated network of tunnels where all the ants live.

TERMITES

Termites are social insects that look and live like ants. They have the most complicated insect societies and build huge nests to live in. The nests can last for several years.

This African termites' nest has umbrellalike layers, but nobody knows why.

BELIEVE IT OR NOT...

The tallest termite nests are made by the African termite. They can measure an amazing 42 ft (12.8 m) high. That's as high as seven tall people standing on top of each other!

Monster Monsters

Some creepers, slitherers, and flutterers are small and sweet-looking, but some are HUGE. Well, that's HUGE when they are sitting next to their small relations. Here are a few of the unbelievably BIG beasties that you really ought to know about.

The Longest Insect
Stick insects are the longest insects in the world. African ones can be as long as 15 3/4 in (40 cm).

The Longest Antennae
The proud owner of the longest antennae is the New Guinea longhorn beetle. Its fantastic feelers are 7 1/2 in (20 cm) long.

The Longest Centipede
At 13 in (33 cm) in length, a centipede found on the Andaman Islands in the Bay of Bengal is the longest one on record. It measured almost 1 1/2 in (4 cm) wide.

Yikes! That's a long, skinny scuttler!

THE LONGEST MILLIPEDE
A kind of millipede from the Seychelles measures as long as 11 in (28 cm).

THE HEAVIEST INSECT
Goliath beetles can weigh up to 3.5 oz (100 g). That's as much as two Funfax books!

THE LARGEST LAND SNAIL
Imagine this if you can. The largest recorded land snail measured 15 1/2 in (39.3 cm) from tip to toe. What a slime trail that slitherer must have left!

THE LARGEST DRAGONFLY
A dragonfly from Central and South America measures up to 4 3/4 in (12 cm) across its wings and 7 1/2 in (19 cm) in length.

THE LARGEST SPIDER
The goliath bird-eating spider is ENORMOUS! One has been found with a leg-span of 11 in (28 cm). Scary, or what?

THE LARGEST BUTTERFLY
The Queen Alexandra's birdwing butterfly is the largest known butterfly in the world. Its wingspan can measure an incredible 11 in (28 cm). Imagine those wings brushing against your face! Aaaagh!

INDEX

Acknowledgments: (KEY: t=top, b=bottom/below, c=center, l=left, r=right) Gary Staab (model-maker): back cover tr

Picture Credits: American Museum of Natural History/OW Myers: 25c; NHPA/Stephen Dalton: 10b; Oxford Scientific Films/Kathie Atkinson: 12c; /Densey Clyne: 13c; /James Robinson: front cover cl.

Additional Photography: Jane Burton, Andy Crawford, Geoff Dann, Angelika Elsebach, Frank Greenaway, Mark Ilcy, Colin Keates, Dave King, Stephen Oliver, Harry Taylor, Jerry Young.

Every effort has been made to trace the copyright holders. Henderson Publishing Ltd. apologizes for any unintentional omissions and would be pleased, in such cases, to add an acknowledgment in future editions.